LET'S VISIT PAKISTAN

Let's visit
PAKISTAN

JOHN C. CALDWELL

BURKE

First published in Great Britain October 1966
Reprinted August 1968
Second revised edition September 1974
Third revised edition 1983
© John C. Caldwell 1966
New material in this edition © Burke Publishing Company Limited 1966, 1974 and 1983

ACKNOWLEDGEMENTS

The publishers are grateful to Garry Lyle for assistance in the preparation of this edition. They would also like to thank the following for permission to reproduce copyright photographs:
    D.A.F.P.; Douglas Dickins; The Government of Pakistan; I.C.A.; Keystone
    Press Agency; Paul Popper Ltd,; Torge Photos; U.S.I.S.
The cover illustration of a market scene in Landi Kotel, a village in the Khyber Pass area, is reproduced by permission of Odhams Press Syndication.

CIP data
Caldwell, John C.
    Let's visit Pakistan. – 3rd Ed. – (Let's visit)
    1. Pakistan – Social life and customs – Juvenile literature
    I. Title   II. Lyle, Garry
    954.9-105   DS379   90179506
    ISBN 0 222 00907 1

Burke Publishing Company Limited
Pegasus House, 116-120 Golden Lane, London EC1Y 0TL, England.
Burke Publishing (Canada) Limited
Toronto, Ontario, Canada.
Burke Publishing Company Inc.
540 Barnum Avenue, Bridgeport, Connecticut 06608, U.S.A.
Printed in Singapore by Tien Wah Press (Pte) Ltd.

Contents

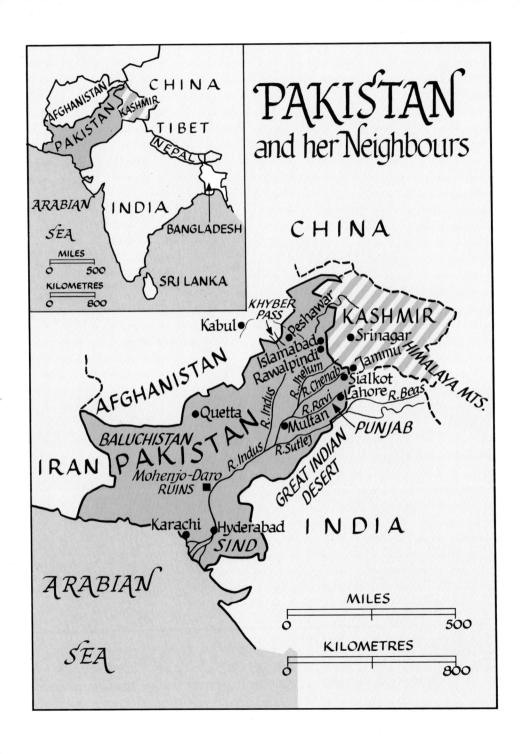

PAKISTAN
and her Neighbours

Inset map
AFGHANISTAN
PAKISTAN
KASHMIR
CHINA
TIBET
NEPAL
ARABIAN
SEA
INDIA
BANGLADESH
SRI LANKA

MILES
0   500
KILOMETRES
0   800

Main map
CHINA

KHYBER PASS
KASHMIR
Kabul
Peshawar
Srinagar
Islamabad
Rawalpindi
Jammu
R. Jhelum
R. Chenab
Sialkot
HIMALAYA MTS.
Lahore
R. Ravi
R. Beas
AFGHANISTAN
Quetta
R. Indus
R. Indus
Multan
PUNJAB
BALUCHISTAN
PAKISTAN
R. Sutlej
IRAN
R. Indus
GREAT INDIAN DESERT
Mohenjo-Daro RUINS
INDIA
Karachi
Hyderabad
SIND
ARABIAN
SEA

MILES
0   500
KILOMETRES
0   800

A Pakistani shepherd boy

Let's Visit Pakistan

Pakistan is one of the several new countries in the continent of Asia. It occupies a little more than one-sixth of the Indian sub-continent. Until 1947 most of the Indian sub-continent was a single country under British rule. Then it became two countries, independent of Britain and of each other. One of the two, the vast central and southern area, kept the name India. The other, carved out of what had been north-east and north-west India, took the new name Pakistan.

This meant that Pakistan was divided into two separate sections. Both were under the same government, even though they were over one thousand miles (over 1,600 kilometres) apart by land or air, and even further apart by sea. If a citizen of West Pakistan travelled to East Pakistan by sea, his voyage covered some three thousand miles (about 4,800 kilometres), or the distance across the Atlantic Ocean. This wide division made it difficult for the people of the two sections to think of themselves as one nation. An even greater difficulty was that they spoke different languages, had different surroundings and interests, ate different food, and even looked different.

Why, then, were they expected to become one nation? The official name of the country—The Islamic Republic of Pakistan—gives a clue to the reason. Islam is the proper name

9

for what we often call Mohammedanism, the religion established by Mohammed. Believers in this religion are called
Moslems, Muslims or Mohammedans. Islam is the religion
of most Arab people who live in the Middle East. It is also the
religion of many of the people of North Africa, Indonesia,
and several other countries. Those other countries include
Pakistan. In 1947, Pakistan had the largest population of
Moslems in the world. So it was hoped that the common
religion would bridge the many differences between the
country's two sections. However, the differences proved too
wide for bridging. In 1971, East Pakistan broke away from

**Islam is the official religion of Pakistan. This picture, taken in
Karachi, shows Moslem worshippers who have removed their shoes
for prayer in accordance with custom**

West Pakistan, to become the independent country of Bangladesh, leaving the old western section as the only Pakistan. That is the Pakistan of today, the country we are visiting. Let's look at the map and find out more clearly where we are.

About 120 miles (200 kilometres) from the Tropic of Cancer, Pakistan faces the Arabian Sea, which forms its southern boundary. It is bounded on the west by Iran (Persia) and on the north by Afghanistan. In the extreme north, a small part of it comes quite close to China. The entire eastern border adjoins India and the territory of Kashmir.

Within these boundaries Pakistan has about 310,000 square miles (800,000 square kilometres) of land which is mainly dry. Rainfall averages from about four to twenty-five inches (ten to sixty-four centimetres) a year, most of it falling in July, August and September. On the coast the weather is usually warm and often very hot. On the inland plains it is very hot in summer and extremely cold in winter. In summer the temperature may sometimes rise as high as 50° C (122° F) during the day and rarely falls below 32° C (90° F) at night. But in the winter, although the temperature may reach 21° C (70° F) during the day, it often falls to freezing-point at night.

The largest river of Pakistan, the Indus, rises in the Tibetan Plateau and is 1,700 miles (2,700 kilometres) long. The Indus is among the most important rivers in Asia. It is especially important to Pakistan, for it flows the whole length of the country, emptying into the Arabian Sea.

Karachi, the former capital and an important seaport, is

11

located near the mouth of the Indus. The Indus and its tributaries provide Pakistan with its water supply. Although rainfall is as low as four inches (ten centimetres) a year in some areas, the river valley soil is rich and fine crops can be grown. The central area of Pakistan is called the Punjab which means "Land of Five Rivers". You will see that five large tributaries— namely the Jhelum, Chenab, Ravi, Beas and Sutlej—flow in a southerly direction before finally uniting to join the Indus. These rivers are connected by long stretches of canal. Some of these canals were built thousands of years ago. At some points there are huge dams to store the water. The precious water from the Indus and the Five Rivers makes the Punjab fertile.

A scene in Kashmir

A Pakistani farmer planting cotton. It is difficult to believe that anything could grow in this sun-baked ground—but it does

There are fields of wheat and cotton, and in some areas there is sufficient water to grow rice.

You will see on the map that some of these important rivers flow through both India and Pakistan. As both countries need plenty of water to grow their crops, it was thought essential at the time of partition in 1947 that the waters of these rivers should be fairly divided. Otherwise, unpleasant disputes might arise.

So, under the auspices of the International Bank for Reconstruction and Development, the water rights of the Indus

Fishermen in Baluchistan making ropes from palm leaves

Baluchi nomads

system of rivers were settled by the signing of the Indus Water Treaty. This treaty was signed by both Pakistan and India on September 19th, 1960.

Broadly speaking, the waters of the three eastern rivers—the Sutlej, Beas and Ravi—are reserved for Indian use and development. The waters of the Chenab, Jhelum and Indus, with its tributaries, are available to Pakistan.

A huge system of dams and canals was needed to replace the waters from the eastern rivers, which formerly irrigated the Punjab and Sind areas of Pakistan. The work is not yet finished but even now Pakistan has one of the world's longest irrigation systems.

Away from the rivers the land is dry and rocky. To the east, the Thar or Indian Desert forms a huge tract along the borders of Pakistan and India. West of the Indus, there is flat desert land which leads into dry, rocky hills. This western area, bordering Iran and Afghanistan, is called Baluchistan. *Istan*

A Baluchi woman from the border country between Iran and Afghanistan. Note her beautiful ornaments; she is wearing a nose-ring as other women might wear ear-rings

A camel train crossing a mountain water-
course. Note the snow-capped peaks in the
background, typical of some of Pakistan's
most beautiful regions

means "the land of" in Persian. Just as Pakistan means "Land
of the Pure", Baluchistan means "Land of the Baluchi People"
and Afghanistan means "Land of the Afghans".

Thus, most of Pakistan is a land of deserts, rocky hills and,
in some areas, beautiful snow-capped mountains. There are
oases scattered through the desert, but extensive farming is
possible only near the Indus River and its tributaries where
there are many irrigation projects and a system of canals which
makes it possible for the otherwise dry land to be farmed.

The highest mountains of Pakistan, called the Hindu Kush,
lie along the northern part of the Pakistan–Afghanistan
border. Mt. Tirich Mir is 25,230 feet (about 7,700 metres)
high, and the Istoro Nal is over 24,000 feet (about 7,300 metres).

The deserts, dry hills and mountains along her western
border cut Pakistan off from her neighbours. There are only a
few passes through which people can travel safely and easily.

17

One of these, called the Khyber Pass, has often been the gateway for invaders who have conquered the Indian sub-continent. The sides of this famous pass are spiked with fortifications, some built centuries ago.

The Khyber Pass begins at a place called Jamrud, about eleven miles (eighteen kilometres) from Peshawar. It then twists and turns for over thirty-three miles (fifty-four kilometres) until it reaches an outpost called Dakha.

Through this fateful pass over the centuries the Persians, the Greeks, the Tartars, the Turks and the Afghans all entered

Some parts of Pakistan are desert. These tribesmen, performing a traditional stick dance in Baluchistan, seem not to notice the intense desert heat

Using bullocks to harvest rice in Sind, one of Pakistan's four provinces

India in turn. They toppled weak empires and founded new dynasties, and left permanent marks on the history of the sub-continent.

Rudyard Kipling, one of the most popular English writers of the late nineteenth century, lived in Pakistan when it was a part of the British colony of India. Several of Kipling's poems tell of battles in the Khyber Pass, or describe the wild mountain tribes who live near by. Later we shall learn more about the invading armies which came through the pass. The rough dry territory into which they descended is now Pakistan's North-West Frontier Province, one of the six government areas into which the country is divided. Four of the six—the North-West Frontier, Punjab, Baluchistan, and Sind—are

A view of Islamabad — Pakistan's new capital built on meadowland in the northern part of the country

provinces, each with its own local government. The other two are administered by the national government, from the newly-built capital Islamabad. Though the national language is Urdu (a language brought to the Indian sub-continent by Moslem invaders) some of these areas have languages of their

20

Most Pakistanis are light-skinned, like this mountain boy

own. For instance, the people of the Punjab speak Punjabi, the people of Sind speak Sindhi, and so forth.

However, most of the 83,000,000 Pakistanis share the same distant ancestors in spite of their different languages. They are of Aryan stock, descendants of a powerful, light-skinned people who came through the Khyber Pass in ancient times. Many Indians are also of Aryan stock. So how is it that two nations with a common ancestry and many common problems can be as different as Pakistan and India? As we shall learn, religion is the greatest dividing factor, and was the reason for the geographical and political division. While Pakistan is predominantly Moslem, India is predominantly Hindu. Religion has probably been the most important single factor in Pakistan's long and unusual history. This history begins in the mysteries of a civilisation which existed almost five thousand years ago.

The Mysterious Past

Our picture shows an ancient city, discovered by archaeologists not many years ago. This city is named Mohenjo-Daro, which means "Mound of the Dead". It is located in the Indus valley, 267 miles (425 kilometres) inland from Karachi. Other similar cities and towns have been unearthed all along the Indus valley.

The ruins of Mohenjo-Daro, a great city built 4,000 years ago

We have no name for the builders of Mohenjo-Daro, other than "the Indus valley people". We do not know whether they were white, brown or black. It is possible that these people were the first to use an alphabet. Many of their inscriptions have been found, but so far scientists have been unable to decipher the writing. Even the exact date when the Indus valley people existed is unknown. Their great cities were probably built between 2500 and 1500 B.C., or about four thousand years ago.

These Indus valley cities were large and well-built. There were numerous two-storey houses. The larger houses had many rooms, including bathrooms. The streets were wide and paved, and most of the buildings were of brick.

These unknown people of Pakistan's remote past had also discovered and used metals; objects made of copper, lead and silver were found in the buried cities. Metal tools have been unearthed, too, as well as ornamental objects.

The manner in which the ancient cities of the Indus valley are built shows that the people were good engineers. The cities are well-planned. They have drainage systems and, even after centuries, we can see that the drains were kept clean. It would appear that the Indus valley cities even had street-cleaning departments!

These vanished people were fine craftsmen. They made figurines and carvings which show elephants, tigers and oxen. The greatest unsolved mystery about them is the distinctive writing carved into pots and on the official seals which must have been used by the government. Many archaeologists have tried to read this script, but the writing is unlike that of any other ancient people.

In fact, even the houses, the tools and the clothing worn by the Indus valley people are different from those of any other ancient civilisation. So many of their cities and villages have been found that we know that there were a good many of these people—perhaps several million. We also know, from the fine buildings and the big granaries where grain was stored, that the Indus valley was a land of great wealth.

Some archaeologists believe that the Indus valley people must have come into what is now Pakistan from some other part of the world. One reason for this belief is that they used metals which are not found in the Indus valley. In addition, they cultivated wheat and raised sheep; but the wheat came from wild grasses, and the sheep from wild sheep, both found only in mountainous areas far distant from the Indus.

There were other large cities in addition to Mohenjo-Daro. Amongst them was Harappa in the Punjab. There was also a more recently discovered city at Kot Diji. They enjoyed a high civilisation for many years. Then, suddenly, the bustling life of these cities came to a stop! We do not know exactly when this happened; but, just as mysteriously as the Indus valley civilisation began, it disappeared. Archaeologists believe that whatever happened to bring this civilisation to an end occurred in about 1500 B.C.

Some scientists think there may have been a great plague

24

A typical farm village in Pakistan. The oxen are valuable beasts of burden

that wiped out the population. Or, more probably, invaders came, killed all the people and moved elsewhere. We may never know the answer to this mystery. We only know that one of the greatest of ancient civilisations suddenly vanished. The Indus valley people died, or were killed, or perhaps moved elsewhere. The great cities were covered by drifting sand, and it is only within the past forty years that they have been dug up. Perhaps some day someone will unlock the secret of the Indus valley by learning to read the script.

Although the people disappeared, some of their achievements lived through the dark ages that followed. The village carts used in parts of Pakistan today are the same, even to the wheel-span, as those of the Indus valley people. Village potters in modern Pakistan use designs similar to those created by the ancient potters of the Indus.

After the Indus valley civilisation disappeared, there was a blank period which lasted for centuries. By this we mean that

25

there are no records to tell us what happened. There are no remains to tell us anything about the people who probably conquered the Indus cities.

It is possible that many invaders came through the Khyber Pass during these centuries. But the first ones about whom we have any facts were the Aryans. It is known that these people began to pour into what is now Pakistan in about 1500 B.C.

The coming of these invaders brings us to the next period of Pakistan's history. This period is one shared by India. During the centuries following the first known invasion from outside, there were no differences between the people of the Indian sub-continent: everyone believed in the religion established by the newcomers, and all people followed similar customs.

Invaders from the North

In about 1500 B.C., wandering tribes from Central Asia and the borderlands between Europe and Asia began to come into the land we know as Pakistan. It is probable that most of these people travelled through the Khyber Pass and into the flat lands along the Indus River. This pass is one of the few ways of crossing the mountains which separate Pakistan and Afghani-

26

stan. It cuts through the Sofed Koh Mountains. The invasions continued for a thousand years.

The newcomers were tall and fair-skinned. They were related to the Greeks, the Persians and the later Romans; and they belonged to the Aryan branch of the human family.

The Aryan nomads spread through what is now Pakistan and moved steadily eastward into the plains of northern India. There were already dark-skinned people called Dravidians living in India. The Aryans drove the Dravidians southward. Sometimes the Dravidians became slaves of the conquerors; at other times relations were peaceful. Many Dravidians still live in southern India.

The invasions from the north came in waves. Sometimes a new wave of Aryans would conquer others who had arrived many years earlier.

In about 518 B.C. a great Persian king called Darius crossed the Himalayan passes and invaded the sub-continent. He made the north-western portion of India a part of his empire.

The Khyber Pass, through which countless invading armies have poured; it has played a crucial role in the history of the Indian sub-continent

Two centuries later, in 326 B.C., Alexander the Great began his campaign in India. A great battle was fought between the Greek and Indian armies on the banks of the River Jhelum. The Indian King Porus was completely defeated. Alexander, encouraged by his victory, advanced as far as the River Beas. But his soldiers were weary and homesick; they yearned for Greece. So Alexander had to turn back. With his return, the Greek rule in northern India ended.

After Alexander's death, the Persians invaded again; they were followed by other people known as Scythians and Kushans. But the dry lands which we know as Pakistan were not as attractive to the newcomers as were the more fertile plains of India. So, while many did settle in what is now Pakistan, many others moved on. In the plains of northern India, the Aryans established many kingdoms and a number of dynasties of Indian or Hindu kings. Remember that at this time, and for centuries to come, India and Pakistan were one.

They were followed by the kings of the Maurya Dynasty— the first powerful line of Hindu kings. Their greatest king was Asoka, who came to power in 274 B.C. For hundreds of years the pattern of history in the Indian sub-continent repeated itself. There would be a powerful dynasty, controlling much of the land; then there would be revolts and war and the founding of smaller, independent kingdoms. The smaller kingdoms would last until the next powerful ruler came to conquer them.

The most important development of this period was that of

the Hindu religion and way of life. We know that religion was to become the great divider in the formation of modern Pakistan and India. It is important for us to know something about Hinduism because the main difference between a modern Pakistani and a citizen of modern India is that of religion.

The Aryan invaders developed a written language called Sanskrit. Twelve of the fourteen most important languages of India were developed from this ancient language. Furthermore, Bengali—the language of Bangladesh—is also derived from Sanskrit.

Through the centuries, the beliefs of Hinduism were written down in Sanskrit in a series of holy books called the Vedas. There are numerous other Hindu books, too, some in the form of poetry, which tell stories of Aryan conquest and which helped to make the Hindu beliefs a vital part of the life of the people. What are these beliefs which have lasted until modern times?

Hindus believe in one Creator, a god whose name is Brahma. There are numerous other Hindu gods, the most important and powerful of them being Vishnu the Preserver, and Shiva the Destroyer. A Hindu worships these and many other gods. He believes that life is filled with evil, and that before attaining perfection a man must be reborn again and again. We call this "reincarnation". As each life is lived, a little of the evil may disappear until, at last, perfection has been achieved. This process might take hundreds of years. At some stage during the many lives, a man might be a lowly

Selling dates in a local market in Pakistan

farmer, be reborn as a merchant, and eventually become a priest or nobleman.

Another important Hindu belief, taught in the Vedas, or sacred books, is that certain animals, especially cattle, are sacred. A good Hindu will eat no meat at all; it is only in very modern times that Hindus have ever eaten beef.

Remember that when the proud and warlike Aryans arrived in India they found the dark-skinned Dravidians. It was partly to separate the invaders from the vanquished that a system called "caste" became an important part of Hindu belief. The Aryans considered themselves superior to the Dravidians, and made rules which divided the two peoples.

It was from this division that the Hindu caste system gradually developed, until eventually all the people belonged to one of the hundreds of different castes many of which continue to this day. At the very top are the Brahmans (also sometimes spelled Brahmins) who are a priestly caste: in Hindu terms, they are thought to have come as near as

30

humanly possible to perfection. In the course of history the Brahmans became very powerful.

Below the Brahmans there are many grades of caste; the people in the lowest caste (Sudra) are called Untouchables. An Untouchable must not be touched by a member of any other caste. He could not, until recent years, worship at a Hindu temple. He could not walk on a public road, and could only be employed in the lowliest and dirtiest jobs.

A member of one caste cannot "graduate" into a higher caste, and members of one caste may not marry or be friendly with members of another. Only death, according to Hindu belief, can change a man's caste. After death, a man may be reborn into a higher caste.

During the earlier centuries of Hindu rule, all the people of the Indian sub-continent shared these beliefs. It was not until the arrival of a wave of new invaders, beginning in the eighth century after Christ, that a new religion began to divide the Indian people. We shall read about this new religion later. For the moment, let's learn about a religion which developed from Hinduism and was to become important in both India and Pakistan.

Siddhartha Gautama, who became known as the Buddha, was a prince who was born in 563 B.C. He believed that man was evil but that purification came, not only through reincarnation, but by practising good deeds and pure thoughts. Buddha did not divide people into castes. Although he was a Brahman and became a great and beloved teacher, he did not

31

Cattle and horses live very close to thatched village houses. In the centre of this compound is a well, with water pots waiting to be filled

consider himself necessarily superior to people of lower caste.

Many Indians became followers of Buddha, including the great Emperor Asoka. Helped by Asoka's interest, the religion of Buddha spread to many other lands. China, Korea, Japan, Cambodia, Burma, Thailand and Sri Lanka are among the Asian nations which are largely Buddhist to this day. And early in its history, Buddhism became a very important religion to the people living in the area we now know as Pakistan. We know this because of ruins which have been found.

The largest collection of ancient Buddhist remains in India or Pakistan are found at Taxila. Near Peshawar there is a small town called Takht Bahi which has the finest Buddhist buildings anywhere in the world.

It is strange that Buddhism has almost died out both in

32

India and in Pakistan. Buddha is still considered a Hindu saint; but, for the most part, the people eventually went back to their Hindu beliefs, although the two religions influenced each other and borrowed from each other. In fact, Buddhism took firmest hold in lands outside India and it still flourishes in many of them. Buddha, who was a modest man, would hardly approve of the huge images in his likeness which are now worshipped in those countries, nor would he approve of the many superstitions now connected with Buddhism.

Of course, the forebears of modern Pakistanis and Indians shared in the development of the Hindu religion and culture, since there was no division between them before the new invaders' religion arrived. Modern Indians and Pakistanis are a mixture of the peoples who lived in the Indian sub-continent

Farmers, taking a break from work, share a communal pipe

centuries ago, and of the many early Aryan invaders who came through the Khyber Pass.

But their history is long, and now we come to the period which divided the people of the Indian sub-continent into Indians and Pakistanis; for new invaders came, bringing a religion so different from Hinduism that the two had difficulty in existing together.

The Moslem Invaders

The prophet Mohammed was born in Mecca, on the Arabian Peninsula, in A.D. 570. Mohammed received revelations from God, and these were written down and preserved in a book called the Koran. The religion established by Mohammed and named after him has become one of the most important in the world. We have mentioned already that believers in this religion are called Mohammedans, Moslems or Muslims, and that the religion is also known as Islam.

Mohammed was a great prophet and followers flocked to his side. Within a few years of his death, there were tens of thousands of Moslems. By the year A.D. 732, just a hundred years after Mohammed's death, fierce Moslem armies had conquered the whole of the Middle East and North Africa, and had even crossed into Spain. They threatened to engulf all Europe. Then, in 732, the Moslem armies were defeated near Poitiers in France. Had this not happened, all Europe might have become Moslem; and it is possible to imagine that both Europeans and Americans might today be followers of this religion. Certainly, the history of the world would have been very different.

For many years even the holy places of the Christian world were controlled by the great Moslem emperors or sultans. The crusades, for example, were fought by European Christians to free Jerusalem from Moslem domination.

Before we learn how the Moslems came to control Pakistan, let's learn about Moslem beliefs. A Moslem believes in one God, who is called Allah. Mohammed was his prophet, and the Koran is the Moslem bible in which Mohammed's revelations from God are preserved. The basic belief can be understood from this sentence from the Moslem creed: "There is no God but Allah, and Mohammed is his Prophet."

Moslems believe in a resurrection and a last judgement. They believe that if a man lives in accordance with the teachings of the Koran, he will attain an after-life in Paradise. The Moslem is democratic in his beliefs; for him, all men are created equal in the sight of God. Moslems reject the caste system, for it creates inequality. Moslems eat all meat except pork; this includes beef, the meat of the animal most sacred

35

to Hindus. Above all, the Moslem has a fierce belief in *one* God, while the Hindu worships many gods.

Both Hinduism and Islam are ways of life which have influenced millions of people. Islam today is not only the religion of the Middle East, but of North Africa, Malaysia and Indonesia. There are millions of Moslems in China also.

Now let's learn how this religion came to India, to produce, in time, two independent and different nations. In A.D. 712, one year after the Moslem armies entered Spain, the Arabs, under their seventeen-year-old leader General Mohammed Bin Qasim, penetrated into the heart of Sind, in what is now Pakistan. He routed the army of the Hindu king and, in A.D. 713, the whole of Sind and the Lower Punjab came under Moslem domination.

For over two centuries, the Moslems were content with these small areas. However, near the end of the tenth century other Moslem warriors began to descend upon India.

In A.D. 998, a king called Amir Sabuktigin crossed from Central Asia and raided Indian territory. With this raid began a series of invasions by Moslem rulers from Central Asia. The greatest of these invaders was Mahmud of Ghazni.

The Hindus fought bravely. They used war elephants, while the Moslems were mounted on fast horses. The elephants were powerful but slow. The mounted Moslem warriors could easily out-distance them.

The Hindus were also weakened by the caste system, for fighting was supposed to be the duty only of members of the warrior caste. Thousands of Hindus were massacred in the battles. Many Hindu temples were destroyed or looted.

Mahmud of Ghazni's men were content with hit-and-run raids. But in 1175 Mohammed Ghori, another Moslem warrior, came with his armies, not merely to loot, but to conquer and stay. By the year 1200, Mohammed Ghori controlled all of what is now Pakistan and much of northern India up to the gates of Delhi. When he died, one of his generals established headquarters at Delhi, and it was from there that Moslem sultans ruled much of India until 1525. In that year another horde of invaders, also Moslems, poured through the Khyber Pass. Babur, chief of the new invaders, was a Moslem Turk, a descendant of both Genghis Khan and Tamerlane. Babur's army numbered only 12,000 men, but within two years he had defeated the armies of the Delhi sultans. Babur then founded the Mogul dynasty, the line of Moslem emperors in India.

The Mogul dynasty became the greatest in Indian history. Akbar, grandson of Babur, ascended the throne in 1556 when he was only thirteen years old. The boy emperor defeated a strong Hindu army and became known as Akbar the Great.

Akbar was a man of great vision. Before his time, Moslem rulers had persecuted Hindus: all Hindus had to pay a special tax, and few Hindus could find employment in the government. Akbar changed all this, for he wanted all his subjects to live together in harmony. He wanted people to be united in common loyalty to their ruler and country. The tax imposed on Hindus was abolished, and they were even able to obtain jobs in the Mogul government. No longer were Hindu temples destroyed and looted.

By 1576, Akbar had become the ruler of the whole of India from the Himalayas down to the middle of the Indian peninsula. His empire was probably the best organised and most efficiently ruled in the world. The empire was divided into a dozen provinces. A just and efficient tax system was established. A royal mint produced coins which were better designed than any in the world at that time. Akbar, who became known as the Grand Mogul, ruled at the time when Queen Elizabeth I was on the English throne. Historians believe that he was just as great and wise a ruler as England's famous queen.

The beautiful Badshahi mosque at Lahore, built by the Mogul emperors

The Taj Mahal
at Agra in India

Unfortunately, the emperors who followed were neither wise nor tolerant. There were many intrigues within the Mogul court. People were heavily and unjustly taxed. The Shah Jehan, Akbar's grandson, began again to levy a special tax on Hindus, and they were often persecuted.

The Moguls were powerful and wealthy rulers and great builders. Shah Jehan was especially interested in architecture. He built the famous Taj Mahal at Agra in India. This beautiful monument was built in memory of his wife Mumtaz Mahal. Twenty thousand workers laboured for twenty-three

39

years to build the Taj Mahal which is often called the world's most beautiful building.

The last powerful Mogul emperor was Aurangzeb who ruled from 1658 to 1707. He was a very staunch Moslem. Having made his part of India into a purely Moslem state, he turned his attention to conquest. For nearly ten years, the armies of Aurangzeb fought against the independent kingdoms of the sub-continent, until he finally conquered them.

Aurangzeb's empire extended from the Himalayas to Cape Comorin, India's most southerly point, and from the Ganges valley to the Indus valley. But the rule was harsh, and revolts broke out. For the last fifteen years of his reign, Aurangzeb was busy leading his huge armies from one part of the country to another. He died, leading his troops, when he was ninety years old.

Although the Mogul court lasted for a hundred and fifty years after Aurangzeb's death, the emperors had little power. As had so often happened in the past, India became divided into scores of small kingdoms. Some were ruled by Moslem kings, others by Hindu rajahs. There was frequent war and revolution; bandits swarmed through the land.

The Moguls were too weak and their land too divided to resist the new invaders who first arrived during the reign of Akbar's son, Jehangir. Before we learn about these newcomers, let's see what effect Moslem rule had on the people.

We have learned that there were periods when Moslems and Hindus lived peacefully together. At other times, the

Moslem rulers persecuted the Hindus, destroyed their temples and imprisoned their priests. The most important effect of Moslem rule was that almost a quarter of the people became Mohammedans. This came about partly through inter-marriage between Moslems and Hindus, and partly because some Hindus were forced to accept the new religion. For the most part, however, Hindus became Moslems voluntarily. Some did so in order to escape the tax on non-Moslems, others in order to get better jobs.

Two areas had the greatest proportion of Moslems. The Indus valley region, which we now know as Pakistan, had many Moslems because the invaders always arrived in this area first. The lower valleys of the Ganges and Brahma-putra, a region known as Bengal, and now partly in Bangladesh, also had a high proportion of Moslems. This area was con-quered by Moslems in 1202; but its ports had also often been visited by Arab ships.

Wherever they lived, Moslems differed from their neigh-bours mainly in religion. It has been said that fewer than ten per cent of Moslems are of "foreign" blood. By this we mean descendants of Arabs, Turks, Afghans or Mogul conquerors.

During the centuries of Moslem rule, the two great re-ligious groups borrowed some ideas from one another. Mos-lems believe in *purdah* for their women. This means that the women live secluded lives, rarely going out. When they do leave their houses, their faces are heavily veiled. Numerous Hindu women accepted *purdah*. In some areas Hindu dietary laws were followed by Moslems. For instance, there are some Moslems who will not eat beef.

Moslem rule affected the Hindu religion too. In some areas, caste almost disappeared, and much of the power of the

The tomb of Jehangir, one of the last Mogul rulers

Brahmans was lost. Some Hindus began to question the caste system, to suggest change. One result of this was the establishment of a new, quite different sect known as the Sikhs.

Sikhs believe in one God and do not believe in caste. A Sikh man never cuts his hair, which is wound into a top-knot. The Sikh covers his head with a turban and always wears a beard.

During the centuries of Moslem rule there were also changes in material ways. The most important of these was in the matter of clothing. The Moslem conquerors came from areas where it was colder than in most of India, so that they had to dress warmly. In addition, they had learned to appreciate beautiful fabrics. We might say that the Hindus began to dress up under the Moslem influence.

The Mogul emperors were great builders. We have mentioned the Taj Mahal, built by the Shah Jehan. Many other royal tombs and beautiful mosques were built during the Mogul rule. (A mosque is a Moslem church.)

We have learned that the language of the Aryan invaders was Sanskrit, and that many modern Indian languages developed from this ancient written language. The Moguls also influenced language when Urdu became the language of the Mogul court. Urdu is written in the Persian script and contains many Persian and Arabic words. Many people began to speak Urdu, or a mixture of Urdu and Hindi called Hindustani.

We have now seen something of how closely the histories

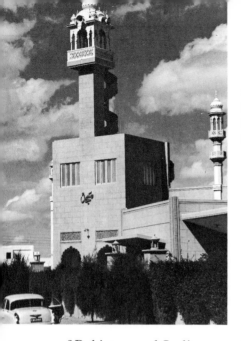

A modern mosque in Karachi. The elaborate tower, which is called a minaret, contrasts rather oddly with the square lines of the building

of Pakistan and India are related. There were periods, lasting for centuries, when the whole of the vast territory followed the Hindu way of life. There were other periods when the Moslems were in power and it was safer to follow Moslem ways.

Religion has always been important here. For some while Buddhism had many followers, and from time to time religious leaders founded new religions. But most people in the Indian sub-continent were either Hindus or Moslems. As we have said, when new invaders came in the seventeenth century, about one person in every four followed the teachings of Mohammed.

Now we will read about the newcomers, and the events which led to the establishment of the two free and independent nations.

44

Spices Lead to British Rule

Plants, especially those which produce things we can eat or fibres which we use in making our clothes, have played an important part in the world's history.

The tea plant, discovered in the hills of southern China seventeen hundred years ago, travelled by ship and caravan to Europe. From Europe, tea went to the New World. Tea, because of the Boston Tea Party, helped to bring about the American Revolution.

Because of cotton and the great plantations which developed in the southern states of America, slavery became profitable. Slavery finally became the issue that started the American Civil War.

In Asia, pepper and other spices such as cloves, nutmeg and cinnamon, changed the course of history. Because of spices, wars were fought; and nations changed their religion. Because of spices, Christopher Columbus and other explorers discovered the Western Hemisphere—they were looking for a short cut to India and the Spice Islands. And because of spices all of southern Asia and most of south-east Asia came under the rule of Europeans.

During the Middle Ages, there was much trade between India and the Ottoman Empire. This was a powerful Moslem empire which controlled most of the Middle East and had its capital in what is now Turkey. During this time the Moslem world and the Christian peoples of Western Europe were bitter enemies. The spices of Asia reached Turkey but got no farther. So it was that Europeans had little with which to flavour their food.

In search of spices, Europe's sea captains defied the belief of most people at the time that the world was flat. They sailed on trips which sometimes lasted for years. And many of the explorers were lost at sea or in some strange or faraway land.

A Portuguese named Vasco da Gama was the first European to reach India. His ships called at the port of Calicut on the south-west coast of India. They picked up a cargo of spices which excited not only the Portuguese. News of Vasco da Gama's cargo spread, and soon many ships were sailing around Africa or trying to reach the land of spices by sailing westward across the Atlantic.

The Portuguese were followed by the Dutch, the British and the French. Each nation tried to establish trading-posts, or factories as they were called. Partly because they were poor

In parts of the subcontinent elephants like this one are still commonly used for heavy work

governors, the Portuguese began to lose ground. The Dutch gained control of the Molucca or Spice Islands (now part of Indonesia). This was one of the factors which caused the British to turn to the mainland of Asia, founding their factories on the coast of India.

Holland was a great seafaring nation in the sixteenth century and, as the Dutch were also good businessmen, they soon gained control of the Spice Islands and the pepper business. In England, meanwhile, in 1600, merchants had banded together to form the East India Company, hoping to take the spice trade from the Dutch or to develop their own factories. As we have said, the British, unable to push the Dutch from the Spice Islands, had turned to the mainland of Asia. They established trading-posts at Bombay on India's west coast and at Madras and Calcutta on the east coast.

The East India Company was an unusual business concern. It had its own army and its own system of government; we might say that it was in partnership with the British government. But the company did not immediately gain control of India. It was not until the Mogul empire began to fall apart after the death of Aurangzeb that the company made much progress. And first it had to fight a series of battles with the Portuguese and the French.

After Aurangzeb's death, the British began to acquire great territory. Often they would make treaties with the many independent Moslem and Hindu rulers who came to power. The rulers would be allowed considerable authority

47

and sometimes they were glad to have British protection.

The British had to fight some wars against Indians too. The Gurkhas, a people living in Nepal, were subdued in 1818. They were forced to sign a treaty giving up certain districts in Bengal. Thereafter, they became great fighters within the British Army. The fierce and warlike Sikhs were defeated in 1849; and the British then became supreme over all India.

The British built a new city called New Delhi, alongside Delhi which was the Mogul capital, and this became the centre of government. In time, the British government took over control from the East India Company, and India became Britain's largest and most important colony. Sir Winston Churchill once said that two out of every ten people in England at one time received their income directly or indirectly from British business in the Indian sub-continent.

We can understand how it was possible for Britain to conquer so many people when we remember that the population of India was divided in itself into Moslems and Hindus, and that the Hindus were further divided into castes. In addition, they were divided by the more than 800 dialects and fourteen main languages which were spoken. India was large in area and in population but weak in unity and leadership.

During the 150 years of their domination of India (called "the British raj"), the British built roads and railways, and established a postal and telegraph system. They also built many schools and hospitals, and opened their own universities to Indian students. But, efficient though the British admini-

Growing rice in an irrigated area

stration was, as with all colonial powers the country tended
to be divided into the rulers and the ruled; and, as more and
more Indians became educated, they began to long for their
own independence.

The names of Mohandas Gandhi and Jawaharlal Nehru
are well known to the world—these men were leaders in
India's fight for independence. But few people can name a
Pakistani who played a major part in this struggle. One reason
for this is that the word "Pakistan" was unknown at that
time—it was only coined as partition drew near. And, for a
long period, the men most active in fighting for independence
were Hindus. This is perhaps because, in the period after the

49

The Persian water-wheel—a primitive method of irrigation still used in Pakistan today. A circle of buckets dips into a well or a river and brings up water which is channelled to the fields

Mogul empire became weak, the Moslems of India lost influence. They were much slower to learn about the new ways and progress brought by the British. Hindus took more quickly to new ideas, and became better businessmen. Moslem religious leaders urged their people to stay away from the new schools. And so, in business, education, medicine and politics, the Moslems lagged behind.

Yet Pakistanis claim that the first real blow for freedom was indirectly struck by Moslems at the time of the Indian Mutiny, as far back as 1857. But while it may well have been the first blow, it also put the Moslem people under a cloud and possibly delayed independence for many years; for the Indian Mutiny, as we shall see, changed the thinking of many Englishmen about eventual freedom for their huge colony.

Independence and Partition

We have already learned how internal conflicts, war and revolts had weakened and destroyed the unity of the country.

The effect of this disunity was to make it easy for foreign powers to conquer the country; when the British and French, who came initially as traders in the early seventeenth century, saw a country politically unstable, they immediately took advantage of the chaotic situation; and the British began steadily and successfully to establish their rule over the whole of the sub-continent.

Yet the Moslems were not to surrender without a struggle. In 1857, they made one final spurt to overthrow the British. This struggle is known in Pakistan's histories as the First War of Independence; in British history it is known as the Indian Mutiny.

Wherever the British ruled they recruited native soldiers to serve in their armed forces. This was also done in India, the locally recruited soldiers being called *sepoys*. As we might suppose, many sepoys were Moslems or Sikhs.

On May 10th, 1857, the sepoys of an army unit in northern India were issued with cartridges coated with a protective grease, and a rumour spread that the grease had been made from pig fat. Most of the sepoys in this particular unit were Moslems. They refused to use the cartridges because Moslems believe that the pig is an unclean animal. As a result, a large

51

number of Moslem troopers were placed under arrest and court-martialled.

Two days later, Moslem troops in Delhi, the old Mogul capital, revolted and pledged their allegiance to the Mogul Emperor Bahadur Shah Zafar. (We have read that the Mogul court still existed although it had very little power.)

The uprising which began on May 10th, 1857, lasted until April 1858. Most of the fighting was confined to northern India. Many battles were fought with great ferocity, bitterness and cruelty. The Moslems fought fiercely but failed in their bid to overthrow the British, who were often aided by provincial dynasties.

They were finally defeated and crushed, and the last Mogul emperor and his family were banished from India.

The British victory was a fatal blow to Moslem power in the sub-continent. The sun now began to set over a people who had ruled India for eight hundred years. The break-up of the Mogul empire was at hand. The Moguls had not only lost their political power; in addition, they were stripped of all prestige and dignity. As a nation, they slipped into a state of political indifference and backwardness.

Because of the war, the Moslem community resisted western ideas for many years. This fact, combined with the effect of the uprising, made them take a back seat in Indian affairs. Efforts to make changes, and to take a greater part in government affairs, were therefore largely left to the Hindus. There were, however, some Moslems who began to play

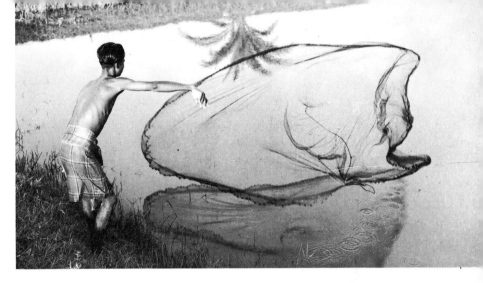

A Pakistani fisherman casting his net in an expert and traditional manner

an important role. One of these was Sir Syed Ahmad Khan.

In 1869 Syed Ahmad Khan visited England and Europe and was much impressed by the progress of European people. When he returned home, he began to tell his people that they must lay aside superstition and age-old ways. He reminded Moslems that Mohammed, their prophet, had said: "Go even to the walls of China for the sake of learning."

Sir Syed (he was knighted by Queen Victoria) founded the famous Aligarh Moslem University. He worked for better relations between Moslems and Hindus. He began to stir his people, and to encourage more and more Moslems to become educated.

However, in spite of Sir Syed's efforts, the leadership in the freedom movement continued for many years to be Hindu. Just before the First World War, Mohandas Gandhi returned

This British-built clock tower is a reminder of the long years of British rule

to India from South Africa. Gandhi had been educated in England and had gone to South Africa to practise law. While there, he had fought for better working conditions for Indians living in that country. He led the Indians in South Africa in peaceful demonstrations of passive resistance to domination, in sit-down strikes, and in what was to become known as "civil disobedience".

Gandhi's methods were very successful in South Africa, and he became a hero when he returned to India. For years he led India's struggle for independence, using the same methods of civil disobedience, of fasting, and of nation-wide strikes which stopped business activities. Gandhi and Nehru became the leaders of the National Congress Party of India, which later became the most powerful political party in the country.

The First World War also created more agitation for freedom among Moslems. During this war, Great Britain fought against Turkey, which was allied with Germany. Turkey was then head of what was known as the Ottoman Empire. Its ruler was called the Caliph, and was considered by all Moslems to be the elected head of the Moslem peoples. Istanbul, capital of the Ottoman Empire, was also the centre of the Moslem world, just as Rome is considered the centre of the Catholic world.

When the Western Allies won the war, all the territories in the Middle East which had been part of the Ottoman Empire were taken away. Moslems everywhere considered the peace terms much too severe. In protest they began what was called the Khilafat Movement. Moslems in India protested to the British against the severe peace terms. Like the Hindus of the Congress Party, they also decided to try non-violent methods of protest. Although the Khilafat Movement did not change the terms of the peace treaty with Turkey, it did serve to unite Moslems against British rule in India.

During these years of struggle, Moslems and Hindus often worked together in India. Numerous prominent Moslems became members of the National Congress Party. Other Moslems worked only through their own organisation, which was formed in 1906 and was called the All-India Muslim League. At first, leaders, whether Moslem or Hindu, thought only in terms of freedom for the whole of India. They did not talk about separate nationhood for Moslems and Hindus.

It was Dr Mohammed Iqbal, a great poet and philosopher, who first suggested an independent Moslem state. Later, Iqbal

A street typical of both India and Pakistan

was joined in this idea by the man whom Pakistanis consider the founder of their nation. His name was Mohammed Ali Jinnah, and he came to be called the *Quaid-i-Azam*, which means "Great Leader".

Jinnah was born in 1876 in Karachi. He completed his school studies at the age of fifteen. Then he went to England to study law, returning to India in 1896 after completing his education. In 1909, at the age of thirty-three, he was elected to the Imperial Legislative Council, and at first he worked unceasingly for Hindu–Moslem unity and constitutional reforms.

Jinnah was a member of the Hindu-dominated Congress Party. But he resigned from it in 1920 when he realised that the policies of the Congress Party were not beneficial to Moslems. Thereafter, he devoted himself entirely to defending and safeguarding Moslem rights.

Jinnah sincerely believed that the future of the Moslems under a Hindu majority rule was dark; he feared that they would always be dominated and that their rights would not be upheld. In 1930, Jinnah decided that there could never be unity and peace between the two great religions. The only hope for the Moslems lay in having a separate homeland of their own, a homeland where they could live according to their own culture and religion, and rule themselves as they had done in the past.

To understand Ali Jinnah's attitude we must understand how bitterness began to grow between the two religious groups. It may seem strange to us, but cows were often the cause of trouble. As we have learned, while the cow is sacred to Hindus, Moslems like beef. Sometimes Moslems would deliberately offend Hindus by making a great to-do over the slaughtering of a cow. Hindus would retaliate by holding noisy festivals and religious ceremonies at the very time when Moslems were worshipping.

Often serious riots broke out between Moslems and Hindus and hundreds of people were killed. Sometimes these riots occurred because Hindus staged noisy processions near mosques. Year after year, the tension between Moslems and Hindus increased. On several occasions, Moslems refused to join in the civil disobedience campaigns started by Gandhi. When Moslem shop-owners refused to close their stores, they were attacked by Hindu mobs.

Meanwhile, the British government had been forced into giving India greater independence, a greater voice in her own government. One of the British concessions was to give the provinces self-government. Members of the provincial legislatures were elected by the people.

Unfortunately, the Congress Party, which had become very powerful, took advantage of these reforms. Moslems became alarmed because the Congress Party was able to control so many elections. In addition, the provincial governments, dominated by the Congress Party, attempted to enforce Hindi as the official language.

Gradually, it became clear that if Britain gave India free-

Cooking chapatties—one of the traditional foods of both Pakistan and India

dom, there must be two new nations based upon religion. In 1933, the name *Pakistan* was first suggested. As we have said, this means "Land of the Pure". But the name was not chosen only for its meaning; rather it came from the initials of some provinces of north-west India which Moslem leaders wanted to be within an independent Moslem state. Thus the "P" stands for Punjab; the "K" for Kashmir; the "S" for Sind, etc.

In the years just before and during the Second World War, the demand for independence increased. The British government offered many different plans which Hindu leaders, or Moslem leaders, or sometimes leaders of both groups, would not accept. Finally, in the middle of the war, the British

A farm in Pakistan

offered complete independence. The only condition was that first the war must be won. As soon as the war was over, British soldiers would leave, and India would be free.

Neither Congress Party nor Moslem League leaders would accept this offer because they felt that winning the war was not relevant. Some of the Hindu leaders, especially Gandhi, turned bitterly against the British.

However, when the Allies finally did win the war, the British kept their promise. Independence and freedom came to India at midnight, August 14th, 1947.

Before the British Parliament granted independence, there were more riots between Hindus and Moslems. There were now many serious problems to be worked out. If freedom was to be granted on the basis of religion, the two parts of the new Pakistan would be separated by a vast stretch of Indian territory. We have already read that the greatest concentrations of Moslems were to be found in the Indus valley in the west and the lower Ganges valley in the east.

There were also many difficult problems in connection with the small princely states. Some of these states were ruled by Hindu rajahs but had Moslem populations; in other states, ruled by Moslems, most of the people were Hindus. For instance, Hyderabad in Central India had a population of 30,000,000. For centuries this rich state had been ruled by Moslems, but most of the population was Hindu. Should Hyderabad be a part of India or a part of the new Pakistan? Indian leaders claimed that Hyderabad should join the new India. However, this state had been a centre of Moslem culture for many years. Moslem leaders naturally wanted it to become a part of their new nation.

On the other hand, the rich state of Kashmir was ruled by Hindu maharajahs, but 85 per cent of its people were Moslems. To make matters more difficult, there was no part of the sub-continent in which all the people were either Moslem or Hindu. There were some Hindus and some Moslems living in every region. If the new nations were to be established entirely on the basis of religion, tens of millions of Moslems and Hindus would have to move and find new houses.

These were some of the problems which faced Mohammed Ali Jinnah (who became the first Governor-General of Pakistan) and the Indian leaders when the two new nations came into existence at midnight on August 14th, 1947. As a result, within a few days, Hindus, Moslems and Sikhs began to murder one another.

Hundreds of villages were burned down; thousands of women and children were kidnapped or murdered. People were butchered simply because of their religion. Hundreds of thousands began to flee for their lives. Hindus who found themselves living in a Moslem state tried to get to Hindu territory. Nearly 7,000,000 Moslems escaped into Pakistan territory.

The killing continued through August, September and October of 1947. It might have ended in war, had not Gandhi started his last fast in order to force Indian leaders to stop the

These Pakistani farmers are celebrating the completion of a road built with American help. The earliest roads in the country were built by the British

campaign against Moslems. Gandhi's fast helped to bring the people, already shocked by the killings, to their senses. But, on January 30th, 1948, a Hindu fanatic, who wanted all Moslems to be killed, assassinated Gandhi.

Hindus and Moslems alike were horrified by the death of Gandhi. Through his civil disobedience campaigns and his fasts, he was in many ways responsible for the freedom which had at last come for Moslems and Hindus alike. He had become a world-famous figure. For thirty years his life had shaped the history of India. In death he made his greatest contribution by causing people to come to their senses. Disagreements still existed, but at least they were faced without bloodshed—or rather without much bloodshed—until 1971.

Now let's learn about the newly created Pakistan, its many problems and its people. Certainly, few nations have become independent in worse circumstances, or paid a heavier price in blood and misery.

Divided Pakistan

Both India and Pakistan faced many unusual problems when they became free and independent nations in 1947. However, the problems of the new Moslem nation of Pakistan were even more difficult than those faced by India.

Pakistan was divided into an eastern section and a western section, with more than one thousand miles (more than 1,600 kilometres) of India between them. The peoples of the two sections had little in common, except the Moslem religion, and were inclined to distrust each other. Their country had no capital and no government buildings. New Delhi, the capital of British India for many years, was now Indian. The large government buildings, and all the files and records of government, were in that city.

The postal system, the telegraph lines, the roads, railways, dams and irrigation canals had been planned for one huge country.

The status of Kashmir, the Hindu-ruled Moslem state to the north of West Pakistan, had not yet been settled. While millions of Moslems had fled from their homes into East and West Pakistan, many more millions still remained in India. Equally well, over ten million Hindus found themselves living in Pakistan. Many people could not afford to flee; others were unwilling to leave villages in which their families had lived for generations.

East Pakistan, while smaller in area, had a larger population than West Pakistan. When Karachi, in West Pakistan, was selected as the national capital, East Pakistanis were angry and apprehensive. After all, there were more people in East Pakistan. Why should the capital be far away in the West?

Karachi was a seaport with 400,000 people, but the population soon grew to over a million. Into this city without

The Empress Market in Karachi. The former capital was built by the British

government buildings came thousands of clerks and officials. For months, tents were used instead of offices, and these were often without desks, telephones or electricity. Often, important government records were lost or had been left in New

Delhi. In addition, tens of thousands of refugees swelled the population of the new capital; they had nowhere to live, and had to be cared for and fed.

There were differences of opinion among the Pakistani leaders as to what kind of government should be developed. Some devoutly religious men wanted to have a strictly Moslem state, with the beliefs of their religion imposed upon all citizens. There were also leaders who wanted Urdu, the principal language of West Pakistan, to be the language of all Pakistan. Naturally, the Bengali-speaking people of East Pakistan did not like this. The East Pakistanis became fearful that, with the government far away in Karachi, they would always be "poor relations" to the West Pakistanis.

Furthermore, for some years after the creation of Pakistan in 1947, no national elections had been held. Politicians were ruining the country by corrupt and inefficient practices. They had little interest in the affairs of the nation. To make matters worse, only one out of every eight Pakistanis could read or write. Economic and social conditions began to deteriorate. High prices, shortage of food and the high cost of living created bitter feelings in the rural areas. In East Pakistan the members of the Assembly had beaten the Speaker and later killed his deputy. In West Pakistan, the Chief Minister had been murdered.

These disturbing conditions aroused fears that Pakistan was on the verge of collapse. Urgent steps were necessary if the nation was to be saved from utter disaster. To save the country from further ruin, General Ayub Khan, the Commander-in-Chief of the army, took over the government of the country on October 7th, 1958. It was one of the most peaceful and bloodless army revolutions in history.

On taking over, the new regime began immediately to root out corruption and malpractice. The capital was moved from Karachi to Rawalpindi, partly so that the government could not be said to be influenced by business interests. The previously forgotten homeless refugees were resettled in new houses especially constructed for them. Massive industrial and agricultural programmes were launched to develop the country and raise the standard of living of the people. The parliamentary government, which until that time had been modelled on the British system, was changed to a presidential form of government with the President as the chief executive.

The President was assisted by a Cabinet of Ministers who, as in the United States of America, were appointed by the President and were not members of the legislature.

The National Assembly consisted of 156 members, divided equally between representatives of East and West Pakistan. Of these, six had to be women. In addition to the National Assembly, East and West Pakistan each had its own elected Assembly.

In the early part of 1965, national elections were held for the first time in seventeen years and Field-Marshal Ayub Khan was re-elected President for another five-year term.

Further evidence of Pakistan's progress was provided by the

fact that, although she proclaimed herself an Islamic republic, there was freedom of worship in the country for all people. The only position which had to be filled by a Moslem was that of the President. Other offices were open to all citizens regardless of race, colour or religious belief.

After Pakistan gained her independence, there were other difficulties to be overcome, besides those connected with the establishment of a strong government. We have mentioned some of these: the fact that so many people were illiterate, for example, and that several million refugees had to be fed and housed. Food shortage was one outstanding question when Pakistan became independent, and it is still difficult to produce enough food for the large population. Also, in one way or another, water is a constant problem.

This brings us to the problem of Kashmir, which has created much tension between Pakistan and India. A huge irrigation system waters over 33,000,000 acres (13,000,000 hectares) of land in Pakistan. The water for Pakistan comes from rivers whose upper reaches are in Kashmir. That is why Kashmir is so necessary to the existence of Pakistan.

A village in Pakistan. Note how parched and arid the land looks

The Tarbela Dam on the Indus River — the world's longest rock-and-earth-filled dam

We read earlier that over eighty-five per cent of the people of Kashmir are Moslems but, at the time of independence, they were ruled by a Hindu maharajah. This is another reason why Pakistan would like to control Kashmir.

How then did India come to control a Moslem state? The intention behind the agreements which led to partition was that the independent states would join India or Pakistan on the basis of the predominant religion of the local inhabitants. Areas where most people were Hindus would become part of India; states where most of the population were Moslems would become a part of Pakistan.

A few months after independence, Moslem tribesmen in Kashmir revolted against the maharajah. They feared that their ruler was going to join Kashmir to India in order to save

69

Moslem herdsmen from the hills of Kashmir

his own position. The Sikh soldiers of the maharajah's army put down the revolt; whereupon many Moslem tribesmen from other areas invaded Kashmir. The invading tribesmen defeated the maharajah's army and pushed forward until they were close to Srinagar, the capital.

The maharajah then asked India for help. The Indian government sent troops by air, and they pushed back the Moslem soldiers and saved the capital for the maharajah. For several months after that, it appeared that there might be war between India and Pakistan over Kashmir. India appealed to the United Nations, accusing Pakistan of aggression because she was helping the Moslem tribesmen who continued to fight India's troops.

The United Nations arranged for a cease-fire in Kashmir. They then recommended a plebiscite, which means that the Kashmir people would put the matter to the vote and so decide for themselves whether to join India or Pakistan. Pakistan agreed to accept the results of a plebiscite; India also agreed, but never put the plebiscite into operation.

Indian soldiers have remained in eastern Kashmir, and the state is now claimed by India. Official Indian maps show it as a part of India. It is interesting to note that Government of Pakistan maps show Kashmir and the smaller state of Jammu as "disputed territory".

There have been many other problems between India and Pakistan, including arguments over the borders between the two countries. Occasionally, Pakistani and Indian soldiers have engaged in border fights; and, in 1971, it seemed that some shooting across the border between India and Pakistan might lead to a full-scale war between the two countries.

The cause of the shooting was a very serious quarrel between the two sections of Pakistan. East and West had still failed to settle their differences. Not satisfied with their own East Pakistan Assembly and an equal share of representatives in the National Assembly, many easterners wanted to govern themselves entirely. They supported a political party called the Awami League, led by Sheikh Mujib ur Rahman. The Awami League won most of the seats in the Assembly at an election in December 1970, and planned to bring in a new constitution which would give East Pakistan complete control over all its own affairs.

By this time, President Ayub Khan had resigned, after riots and violent demonstrations which the government could not control. His place had been taken by President Yahya Khan, another westerner. President Yahya Khan tried to block the Awami League by delaying a meeting of the Assembly. That

71

led to more riots, as well as strikes and demonstrations through-
out Pakistan. Fearing an armed rebellion, the President then
declared martial law, and ordered the army to put down the
disturbances. Sheikh Mujib was imprisoned, but his followers
resisted the army. They declared that East Pakistan was now an
independent state, with the name Bangladesh. And in a brief
but bitter and very destructive war they forced the government
to let them have their own way. The old West Pakistan is now
the only Pakistan and is once more partly under military rule.

This has been so since 1977 when riots following an election
were so violent that the army took over the government
and put General Zia-ul-Haq is charge. General Zia has since
been declared President and he rules through a council of
mainly civilian advisors. The council has announced that it is
gradually preparing for democratic elections.

Not the least of any Pakistan government's problems is the
country's relations with India.

During the war, about 8,000,000 East Pakistanis who had
lost their homes or felt in danger of losing them took refuge over
the border, in India. Pakistan believed that India was arming
some of these refugees, and helping them to make guerilla
warfare on the government army. That caused the border
shooting which for a time seemed likely to bring India into the
war on the side of Sheikh Mujib's followers. It has also caused
further suspicion and dissension between India and Pakistan
since the war ended, especially as India has remained on
friendly terms with Bangladesh.

However, if Pakistan is to play to the full her part as one of the largest Moslem nations in the world, she must have better relations with her neighbours. India and Pakistan working together could solve their problems and could give their nations a more important voice in world affairs. It is to be hoped that the bitterness of the past can eventually be forgotten. The Moslems and Hindus who have shared so many centuries as one people can surely live in friendship and peace once more.

Living in Pakistan

Now let's learn about life in modern Pakistan. How do people live in the cities and in the country? What food is eaten, and what clothes are worn?

If you were a boy living in Pakistan, your first name might be Mohammed, sometimes spelled Muhammed. This is one of the most common boy's names among Moslems. Indeed, wherever there are Moslems, whether it be in the Middle East or Indonesia, there are boys named Mohammed. Other common names are Ali, Ahmed, Amin and Husain (spelled Hussein in the Middle East).

Because they are Moslems, Mohammed, his friends and their

families would pray five times each day. As they pray, they would bow in the direction of Mecca. This is the city in Saudi Arabia where Mohammed the Prophet is buried. Mecca is holy to all Moslems; no matter where they may be or what they may be doing, the faithful turn toward Mecca in prayer five times a day.

The call to prayer is given from a minaret or tower which is often part of a mosque. Mohammed, his friends and their families would often go to the mosque to hear the word of God as read from the Koran. They would celebrate Ramadan, a

Boys at school in Pakistan

religious festival: for a month, they would be fasting from sunrise to sunset each day.

There are several sects or denominations among Moslems. Mohammed and his friends might belong to different sects, but their main beliefs would be the same. As good Moslems they would hope some day to visit Mecca, the Holy City. It is the hope of all devout Moslems, wherever they may live, to go on this pilgrimage. However, most Pakistanis never manage to do so. You can see from the picture of a typical house that the standard of living is still fairly low and, although a pilgrim can visit Mecca very cheaply, the cost is more than many people can afford.

Apart from the standard of living, climate has much to do with the construction of houses in Pakistan. If he lived in a rural area, Mohammed's house would be made of hardened clay or mud bricks. It might have a thatched roof, but a flat tile or mud roof would be more likely. These houses are small, often rectangular in shape. They have very little furniture. Mohammed and his brothers and sisters might have to sleep on the floor.

We know that Pakistan has a hot, dry climate, which is unsuitable for growing some of the more common crops of Asia. Mohammed and his family like rice. However, this food can only be served on very special occasions. Wheat, which is grown in the irrigated fields of the Punjab, is Pakistan's most important source of food.

Wheat is used in various ways. Mohammed's mother will

A village scene—houses are small and crowded and much of the life is carried on in the open air

often make *chapatties*, which are thin, unleavened pancakes. With the chapatties there will be meat and vegetables, often cooked with curry powder.

Curry is a very popular hot spice flavouring in Pakistan and India, and curried vegetables and meat are common dishes. We know that good Moslems may not eat pork. Mohammed's family, therefore, do not eat pork at all; of the meat available to them they like mutton more than beef. Some Pakistanis have an idea that beef is hard to digest. However, it is often eaten because it is less expensive than mutton.

Mohammed's mother may also make *kebab*. This is barbecued mutton, cooked with many spices; it is very good. Whatever the meal may be, Mohammed and his family will eat with their fingers. There are no knives and forks, nor do they use chopsticks as in China or Japan. Eating with one's fingers is not as messy as you may think. The chapatties are used to pick up and hold bits of meat and vegetables, so that a sort of bite-sized sandwich is made which is popped into the mouth.

76

Our illustrations include several pictures which show the kind of clothing worn in Pakistan. Pakistani clothing is loose-fitting, often white. Sometimes the men and boys wear shorts, but the baggy, pyjama-like trousers, called a *shalwar*, are more common. A shirt is worn with these loose trousers and, if a man is dressed for a special occasion, a long high-collared coat, called a *sherwani*, is worn. You may have noticed too that in almost all the pictures the men are wearing turbans. Turbans are often wound around a skull cap called a *kulla*.

If Mohammed lives in the Punjab, he will tie his turban

Oxen thresh wheat by trampling it underfoot

differently from the way it is tied in other parts of Pakistan. In fact, it is almost always possible to know what area a man is from by the way in which his turban is tied.

Mohammed's mother will probably wear a *shalwar* too. And with it she will wear a shirt called a *kamiz*, and a shawl called a *duputta* which covers the shoulders and goes over the head. For special occasions, a beautiful *sari* may be worn. This is a long length of silk or cotton, always in a lovely colour, which is wound around the waist, and then drawn up around the shoulders or over the head. Women in Pakistan also often wear a kind of divided skirt called a *gharara*.

We have used the word *purdah* elsewhere in this book. Perhaps Mohammed's mother may live in purdah. This means that if guests come she stays in the kitchen, or in her own room if the house is large enough for her to have one. When she goes to market, or out in the street for any reason, she covers her face with her *duputta*. Traditional Moslems believe that a woman's place is at home, that she should be very modest, and that she should always cover her face in the presence of any men except those of her family.

Pakistani schoolgirls. Note that one is heavily veiled

However, times are changing in Pakistan. If Mohammed has an older sister, she may go to school, and she probably does not live in purdah. Pakistani girls are learning to be nurses, doctors, even air hostesses.

We can get some idea of how much things are changing in modern Pakistan from the numbers of children, both boys and girls, who now go to school. Mohammed's father and mother probably never went to school at all, and can neither read nor write. Illiteracy is one of Pakistan's greatest problems; but everywhere there are new schools being built, and soon schooling will become compulsory for all children.

In school, Mohammed would study many of the subjects studied in European schools. There would be history, geography and arithmetic. The major difference between Mohammed's school and those in other countries is in the languages which must be studied. If Mohammed lives in the Punjab he will speak Punjabi, and his written language will probably be Urdu. However, if he lives in Sind, which is south of the Punjab, he will speak Sindhi, and his written language will also be Urdu. Wherever he lives in Pakistan, he will begin school in Urdu, because Urdu is the national language of Pakistan, and is used in schools.

From our picture we can see how Mohammed might write the Urdu alphabet. There are thirty-eight letters or sounds in this way of writing. Instead of beginning on the left-hand side of the page as we do in English, Mohammed will begin on the right. As we have said, Urdu is written in Persian script and

79

can also be read by the people of Persia—or Iran as we now call that country.

Because of the many curves and squiggles, it is difficult to write Urdu properly with a modern pen. Mohammed will use a pen or stylus made from a special kind of reed which grows in swampy places along the Indus River. After he has learned to write the flowing Urdu letters, he will discover that in his language there is a sort of shorthand. When letters are put together to form words, they are often shortened. Some of the dots and squiggles are left out.

After learning Urdu, Mohammed must also study English, which is the second language in Pakistan. In some secondary schools and colleges, English is used in teaching almost all subjects.

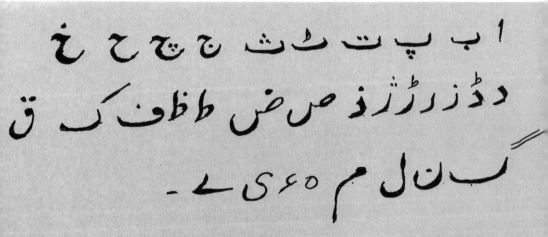

A caravan of Bactrian or mountain camels

The English language is very important in Pakistan: it is the language of business, many newspapers and magazines are published in English, and many Pakistanis can speak to one another only in English because their own languages are so different. Of course, now that everyone also studies Urdu, this language will soon become a means of communication for all the people in Pakistan, and it is expected that English will become less important as time goes by.

Since Pakistan is a poor country, Mohammed will have to walk to school. There are very few school buses, but there are many fine roads through the generally flat countryside. And there are some ordinary buses and trains. However, Mohammed and his family, being average folk, would probably travel to market or visit friends in a bullock cart, or *tonga*.

Notice the camels in our picture. Camels pull carts in

A camel cart in the middle of one of Pakistan's largest cities

Pakistan, and are sometimes used for ploughing or for turning the wheels of flour mills. There are two kinds of camels. One has short hair. The other is shaggy and is called the Bactrian, or mountain, camel. Oxen are even more important than camels as beasts of burden; oxcarts are used in many sections of Pakistan. The dung from oxen and camels is used for fuel in most homes, since there are few trees and most people cannot afford to buy wood or coal. Fortunately, because the

82

climate is hot except in the mountains, a fire is necessary only for cooking.

If Mohammed's family is typical, they will live in the country or in a small village. About eighty per cent of the Pakistani people live by farming. But there are some large cities in Pakistan. Karachi, the former capital now has a population of over four million. It is a city of wide streets and many new buildings. Even here, though, there are many camel carts. The camels often wear bells on their knees and flowers in their harnesses.

The Shalimar Gardens, Lahore

In the picture of the market-place you can see the different methods of transportation used in Karachi. Near the clock-tower there are taxis and buses. Near the centre of the picture there is a camel cart and a horse-drawn carriage called a *gharry*. In the foreground there are several pedicabs or rick-shaws. A bicycle is used to pull this almost-square two-wheeled vehicle.

Karachi lies north-west of the mouth of the Indus River. It is the largest city in Pakistan, and is famous for its natural harbour and its international airport. Ships from Europe,

A market place in Karachi which shows clearly the contrast between ancient and modern, both in the surrounding buildings and in the various types of vehicles

America and the Far East call at Karachi. Its airport is busy, with modern jet airliners landing and taking off day and night, bringing Karachi within a few hours' of most of the capitals of the world. Because it was once the capital, Karachi became the nerve centre of the business, commercial and industrial world; and though the importance of Karachi has since diminished, it still continues to conduct the country's big business.

Rawalpindi, another big city, is situated in the northern part of Punjab, near the famous snow-capped hills of Murree. It replaced Karachi as the temporary capital until the new capital, Islamabad, was completed in 1967. Islamabad, which took six years to build, stands on the dark brown Potwar Plateau not far from Rawalpindi. It is still a very small city but it is one of the most modern capitals in Asia.

Now we come to Lahore, the second largest city in Pakistan. It has a population of well over 2,000,000. Lahore is 811 miles (about 1,300 kilometres) away from Karachi and is an important religious and educational centre.

This city was a favourite of the Mogul emperors. They planned some of the loveliest gardens and built some of the country's most famous mosques and mausoleums there. The beautiful Shalimar Gardens with their pools and fountains, and the mausoleum of Emperor Jehangir, still attract innumerable tourists. The Mogul emperors also built the world's largest mosque, called Badshahi, which is a most impressive sight with its many high arches and huge marble domes.

A view of modern Lahore, a city of wide traffic-filled streets and impressive buildings as well as some of the country's most famous ancient mosques and mausoleums

From Lahore we cross the country to Peshawar. Here the people are mainly Pathans, a brave and warlike people who have lived near the Khyber Pass for centuries.

These people who live among the mountains of Pakistan, are different from those of the desert and the plains. In the mountains, there are many herdsmen; the job of a mountain boy may be to care for the sheep and goats. More clothing must be worn in the mountains, for there is often frost and snow. Yet in some of the mountain valleys rice can be grown, because they are sheltered from the cold and have a much higher rainfall than the rest of Pakistan.

The mountains are among the highest and roughest in the world, and so bring many foreign mountaineers to Pakistan. The Pakistanis themselves have not yet produced a great climber, but they do love games and are good athletes. The most popular games are cricket, hockey, squash and soccer. Pakistan's hockey teams have won Olympic medals. And their cricket team has been known to beat England in Test matches.

Pakistanis love to fly kites. They have interesting kite-flying contests. The kite strings are covered with glue and ground glass. Each boy tries to force his kite string against those of other boys in such a way that the strings will be cut by the glass.

Perhaps it is kite-flying which makes many Pakistanis interested in aircraft. There is never a shortage of good pilots and aircraft technicians in Pakistan, and aircraft are used more and more to carry passengers and goods over the long

A water-carrier—a familiar scene in Pakistan where many areas are never far from drought

distances within the country. The government also operates a fine airline called Pakistan International Airlines, whose big jets may be seen at most of the world's airports.

Pakistan Develops

Supplying food for a large and growing population is Pakistan's most urgent problem. Even though eight out of ten Pakistanis live by farming, their work does not produce enough food to go round. Indeed, there are many farmers who cannot always produce enough to feed their own families. So Pakistan, with all its farmland must import vast quantities of food each year to keep her population from hunger.

One reason for this is the nature of the country. With a low average rainfall in the best of years, much of the farmland is never very far from drought—and drought, of course, means poor crops or sometimes no crops at all. On the other hand, farmers in the long, low-lying river valleys are often troubled by too much water. When there are heavy rains or sudden thaws of snow in the mountains to the north, the rivers come down in flood, washing crops and topsoil away, and leaving fields waterlogged. Also, much farmland in the river valleys is spoiled because the very hot sun causes quick evaporation. This takes the necessary moisture from the soil, but leaves deposits of salt in which crops cannot grow.

Another reason is that many Pakistani farmers do not grow food crops. They grow cotton to supply the weaving mills which keep many town-dwelling Pakistanis in employment, and to meet export orders from countries like Britain, which make cotton goods but do not grow the raw material. Developing countries need town industries and the money that can be earned from exports, so Pakistan cannot do without her cotton crops. However, she would be a much stronger country if she could grow them without relying on other countries for so much of her food supply.

Yet another reason for the food problem is the way in which the land is shared and treated—or rather the way in which it *was* shared and treated. Until recently, a great deal of the land was held by a fairly small number of rich people. They could stay rich without trying to make their land more productive, and so they left large areas idle or unimproved while many other people could not find enough farmland to keep them at

Mechanical handling and transport aids often contrast with traditional dress, as is shown here

work for more than one third of the year. Some farmers had to make do with less than one acre (about one-half hectare), and even in the well-watered Five Rivers area a Pakistani farmer needs at least $12\frac{1}{2}$ acres (about five hectares) to make a living.

However, there have been some big changes since West Pakistan became the only Pakistan. At that time, many West Pakistanis were nearly as discontented with their government and their standard of living as the East Pakistanis who had rebelled. Also, the country had lost a market as well as an important source of income and supplies when the rebellion won independence for the easterners. So when democratic government was restored, in 1972, its first task was to help the farming people and to make the farmland more productive.

A task of that kind cannot be completed in a month or two, nor even in a year or two. But it is clearly on the way to

90

success. Perhaps 1,000,000 acres (405,000 hectares) of land have been taken from those who had too much and given to farmers who had too little, or to landless people who wished to become farmers. Farmers who had been too poor to buy fertilisers, pest-killers, machinery and better types of seed may now have them, and are being taught to use them. Irrigation is being extended. Land made useless by erosion or by salt deposits is being reclaimed. Better roads, more comfortable houses and new markets are being provided. Social welfare services for farmers' families have begun. And the results must soon show in a better-fed people who rely less and less on imported food.

In all this rural improvement, the Pakistanis have had much good advice and practical help from the Food and Agricultural Organisation of the United Nations. They have

Improved social conditions in Pakistan include medical services and hospitals such as the one in which this photograph was taken

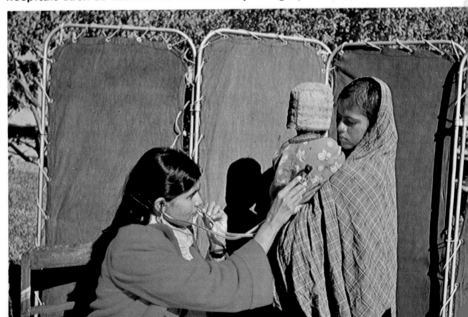

With other changes, Pakistan is introducing better training facilities for doctors. This is a medical college for women in Lahore

also been helped by individual nations, particularly the United States, Britain and some other countries of the Commonwealth. Pakistan was herself a member of the Commonwealth until disagreement over the East Pakistan troubles caused her to withdraw. However, she has remained on friendly terms with most Commonwealth countries, and Britain is still an important market for her raw cotton and her factory products.

In the modern world, no nation can be strong without factory industries, and while her farmers are learning to grow more food, Pakistan is also developing these industries. Indeed, she has been able to develop them more quickly and

92

more successfully than she has developed her farmland. When she was part of British India, the whole country had only thirty-four factories. Most were very small, and apart from the cotton mills they produced mainly for the home market. But the factories of Pakistan now number more than 1,200. Many compete in the world markets with such exports as cloth, cement and sporting goods, while others produce a wide range of goods for local use. These include sugar and other foods, fertilisers, bicycles, sewing machines, tools, paint, paper and chemicals. There are also steel foundries, oil refineries and a very busy shipbuilding yard.

Many of these industries were begun and developed under three "five-year plans" which spread over the years from 1955 to 1970, but they suffered a severe setback during the time when East Pakistan was struggling to become Bangladesh. Even when peace and democratic government were restored some industries were slow to pick up, and in 1972 the government took control of those on which other industries depended. Steel production, motor vehicle assembly, oil refining, heavy engineering and the manufacture of fertilisers and other important chemicals all became national industries.

Since then, and with help from China as well as from her older friends, Pakistan has again expanded her factory industries. She has also begun to extend her transport and other service industries, and not only within the country. As examples, many foreign shipping companies are sending their vessels for repair and refitting in the big shipyards at Karachi, and the international air service called Air Malta is not quite what it sounds. Though based in Malta and controlled by the Malta Government, it was provided and is managed by Pakistan International Airlines.

But there is one problem which neither industrial progress nor higher standards of living can solve. If Pakistan is to play her part as a leading Moslem nation and one of the strongest developing nations she must have better relations with her huge neighbour India and her one-time partner Bangladesh. It is not too much to hope that relations will improve. Pakistan took a welcome step by recognising Bangladesh as a separate and independent nation. She has already gone some of the way towards settling her differences with India. So the three nations may yet decide that they can work together for the good of the sub-continent that they share. By working together, they can overcome their difficulties, and each can become more prosperous and play a fuller part in world affairs.

Another contrast seen in modern Pakistan. These men and the camel are standing near flares burning waste gas from a huge natural gas field.
Pakistan today is trying to make use of all her natural resources to improve the economy of the country

Index